THE LIGHT
AROUND
THE BODY

ROBERT BLY

THE LIGHT AROUND THE BODY

HarperPerennial

A Division of HarperCollinsPublishers

Acknowledgment is made to the following magazines in which some of these poems have previously appeared: *The Nation, Choice, The San Francisco Review, Paris Review, Kayak, The Sixties, It, American Dialog, East Side Review, Chelsea, New World Writing, Polemic, Some/Thing, Coastlines,* and *Unicorn Broadsheets.* The following poems were published in *Poetry:* "Written in Dejection near Rome" (under the title "Written near Rome"), "A Journey with Women," "At a March against the Vietnam War" (under the title "March in Washington"), "Those Being Eaten by America" (under the title "The Life of Weeds"), "A Dream of Suffocation" (under the title "An American Dream"), "Smothered by the World" (under the title "The Testament"), "A Home in Dark Grass" (under the title "Poem in Praise of Solitude"), "The Current Administration" (under the title "The Confusion of America"), "Suddenly Turning Away," "The Hermit," "Looking at Some Flowers," "Come with Me," "Riderless Horses," "Hurrying Away from the Earth," and "When the Dumb Speak."

A hardcover edition of this book was published by Harper & Row, Publishers, Inc.

First Harper Colophon edition published 1985. First HarperPerennial edition published 1991.

Library of Congress Cataloging-in-Publication Data

Bly, Robert.
    The light around the body.

    (Harper colophon books)
    Reprint Originally published: London :
Rapp & Whiting, 1968.
    I. Title.
[PS3552.L9L5   1985]   811'.54   84-48640
ISBN 0-06-090786-X (pbk.)

91 92 93 94 95 CW 10 9 8 7 6 5 4 3 2

FOR MY *mother* AND *father*

Contents

IV. IN PRAISE OF GRIEF

V. A BODY NOT YET BORN

I

The Two Worlds

For according to the outward man, we are in this world, and according to the inward man, we are in the inward world. . . . Since then we are generated out of both worlds, we speak in two languages, and we must be understood also by two languages.

—Jacob Boehme

The Executive's Death

Merchants have multiplied more than the stars of heaven.
Half the population are like the long grasshoppers
That sleep in the bushes in the cool of the day:
The sound of their wings is heard at noon, muffled, near the
    earth.
The crane handler dies, the taxi driver dies, slumped over
In his taxi. Meanwhile, high in the air, executives
Walk on cool floors, and suddenly fall:
Dying, they dream they are lost in a snowstorm in mountains,
On which they crashed, carried at night by great machines.
As he lies on the wintry slope, cut off and dying,
A pine stump talks to him of Goethe and Jesus.
Commuters arrive in Hartford at dusk like moles
Or hares flying from a fire behind them,
And the dusk in Hartford is full of their sighs;
Their trains come through the air like a dark music,
Like the sound of horns, the sound of thousands of small wings.

The Busy Man Speaks

Not to the mother of solitude will I give myself
Away, not to the mother of love, nor to the mother of conversation,
Nor to the mother of art, nor the mother
Of tears, nor the mother of the ocean;
Not to the mother of sorrow, nor the mother
Of the downcast face, nor the mother of the suffering of death;
Not to the mother of the night full of crickets,
Nor the mother of the open fields, nor the mother of Christ.

But I will give myself to the father of righteousness, the father
Of cheerfulness, who is also the father of rocks,
Who is also the father of perfect gestures;
From the Chase National Bank
An arm of flame has come, and I am drawn
To the desert, to the parched places, to the landscape of zeros;
And I shall give myself away to the father of righteousness,
The stones of cheerfulness, the steel of money, the father of rocks.

Johnson's Cabinet Watched
by Ants

1

It is a clearing deep in a forest: overhanging boughs
Make a low place. Here the citizens we know during the day,
The ministers, the department heads,
Appear changed: the stockholders of large steel companies
In small wooden shoes: here are the generals dressed as gam-
    boling lambs.

2

Tonight they burn the rice-supplies; tomorrow
They lecture on Thoreau; tonight they move around the trees,
Tomorrow they pick the twigs from their clothes;
Tonight they throw the fire-bombs, tomorrow
They read the Declaration of Independence; tomorrow they are
    in church.

3

Ants are gathered around an old tree.
In a choir they sing, in harsh and gravelly voices,
Old Etruscan songs on tyranny.
Toads nearby clap their small hands, and join
The fiery songs, their five long toes trembling in the soaked
    earth.

Watching Television

Sounds are heard too high for ears,
From the body cells there is an answering bay;
Soon the inner streets fill with a chorus of barks.

We see the landing craft coming in,
The black car sliding to a stop,
The Puritan killer loosening his guns.

Wild dogs tear off noses and eyes
And run off with them down the street—
The body tears off its own arms and throws them into the air.

The detective draws fifty-five million people into his revolver,
Who sleep restlessly as in an air raid in London;
Their backs become curved in the sloping dark.

The filaments of the soul slowly separate:
The spirit breaks, a puff of dust floats up,
Like a house in Nebraska that suddenly explodes.

Smothered by the World

Chrysanthemums crying out on the borders of death,
Lone teeth walking in the icy waters,
Once more the heavy body mourns!
It howls outside the hedges of life,
Pushed out of the enclosure.
Now it must meet the death outside the death.
Living outside the gate is one death,
Cold faces gather along the wall,
A bag of bones warms itself in a tree.
Long and bitter antlers sway in the dark,
The hairy tail howls in the dirt . . .

A Dream of Suffocation

Accountants hover over the earth like helicopters,
Dropping bits of paper engraved with Hegel's name.
Badgers carry the papers on their fur
To their den, where the entire family dies in the night.

A chorus girl stands for hours behind her curtains
Looking out at the street.
In a window of a trucking service
There is a branch painted white.
A stuffed baby alligator grips that branch tightly
To keep away from the dry leaves on the floor.

The honeycomb at night has strange dreams:
Small black trains going round and round—
Old warships drowning in the raindrop.

Romans Angry about the Inner World

What shall the world do with its children?
There are lives the executives
Know nothing of,
A leaping of the body,
The body rolling—and I have felt it—
And we float
Joyfully on the dark places;
But the executioners
Move toward Drusia. They tie her legs
On the iron horse. "Here is a woman
Who has seen our mother
In the other world!" Next they warm
The hooks. The two Romans had put their trust
In the outer world. Irons glowed
Like teeth. They wanted her
To assure them. She refused. Finally they took burning
Pine sticks, and pushed them
Into her sides. Her breath rose
And she died. The executioners
Rolled her off onto the ground.
A light snow began to fall
And covered the mangled body,
And the executives, astonished, withdrew.
The other world is like a thorn

In the ear of a tiny beast!
The fingers of the executives are too thick
To pull it out!
It is like a jagged stone
Flying toward them out of the darkness.

II

The Various Arts of Poverty and Cruelty

When we think of it with this knowledge, we see that we have been locked up, and led blindfold, and it is the wise of this world who have shut and locked us up in their art and their rationality, so that we have had to see with their eyes.

—Boehme

Our fathers ate manna in the wilderness and they died.

—Old liturgy

What a distressing contrast there is between the radiant intelligence of the child, and the feeble mentality of the average adult.

—Freud

Come with Me

Come with me into those things that have felt this despair for
    so long—
Those removed Chevrolet wheels that howl with a terrible lone-
    liness,
Lying on their backs in the cindery dirt, like men drunk, and
    naked,
Staggering off down a hill at night to drown at last in the pond.
Those shredded inner tubes abandoned on the shoulders of thru-
    ways,
Black and collapsed bodies, that tried and burst,
And were left behind;
And the curly steel shavings, scattered about on garage benches,
Sometimes still warm, gritty when we hold them,
Who have given up, and blame everything on the government,
And those roads in South Dakota that feel around in the dark-
    ness . . .

Those Being Eaten
by America

The cry of those being eaten by America,
Others pale and soft being stored for later eating

And Jefferson
Who saw hope in new oats

The wild houses go on
With long hair growing from between their toes
The feet at night get up
And run down the long white roads by themselves

The dams reverse themselves and want to go stand alone in the
    desert

Ministers who dive headfirst into the earth
The pale flesh
Spreading guiltily into new literatures

That is why these poems are so sad
The long dead running over the fields

The mass sinking down
The light in children's faces fading at six or seven

The world will soon break up into small colonies of the saved

Written in Dejection

near Rome

What if these long races go on repeating themselves
century after century, living in houses painted light colors
on the beach,
black spiders,
having turned pale and fat,
men walking thoughtfully with their families,
vibrations
of exhausted violin-bodies,
horrible eternities of sea pines!
Some men cannot help but feel it,
they will abandon their homes
to live on rafts tied together on the ocean;
those on shore will go inside tree trunks,
surrounded by bankers whose fingers have grown long and
    slender,
piercing through rotting bark for their food.

Listening to President Kennedy Lie
about the Cuban Invasion

There is another darkness,
A darkness in the fences of the body,
And in moles running, and telephone wires,
And the frail ankles of horses;
Darkness of dying grass, and yellow willow leaves;
There is the death of broken buttonholes,
Of brutality in high places,
Of lying reporters,
There is a bitter fatigue, adult and sad.

The Great Society

Dentists continue to water their lawns even in the rain;
Hands developed with terrible labor by apes
Hang from the sleeves of evangelists;
There are murdered kings in the light-bulbs outside movie thea-
  ters;
The coffins of the poor are hibernating in piles of new tires.

The janitor sits troubled by the boiler,
And the hotel keeper shuffles the cards of insanity.
The President dreams of invading Cuba.
Bushes are growing over the outdoor grills,
Vines over the yachts and the leather seats.

The city broods over ash cans and darkening mortar.
On the far shore, at Coney Island, dark children
Play on the chilling beach: a sprig of black seaweed,
Shells, a skyful of birds,
While the mayor sits with his head in his hands.

Suddenly Turning Away

Someone comes near, the jaw
Tightens, bullheads bite
The snow, moments of intimacy waved away,
Half-evolved antennas of the sea snail
Sink to the ground.
The sun
Glints on us! But the shadows
Of not-love come.
It cannot be stood against.
And we suffer. The gold discs
Fall from our ears.
The sea grows cloudy.

Three Presidents

Andrew Jackson

I want to be a white horse!
I want to be a white horse on the green mountains!
A horse that runs over wooden bridges, and sleeps
In abandoned barns. . . .

Theodore Roosevelt

When I was President, I crushed snails with my bare teeth.
I slept in my underwear in the White House.
I ate the Cubans with a straw, and Lenin dreamt of *me* every
    night.
I wore down a forest of willow trees. I ground the snow,
And sold it.
The mountains of Texas shall heal our cornfields,
Overrun by the yellow race.
As for me, I want to be a stone. Yes!
I want to be a stone laid down thousands of years ago,
A stone with almost invisible cracks!
I want to be a stone that holds up the edge of the lake house,
A stone that suddenly gets up and runs around at night,
And lets the marriage bed fall; a stone that leaps into the water,
Carrying the robber down with him.

John F. Kennedy

I want to be a stream of water falling—
Water falling from high in the mountains, water
That dissolves everything,
And is never drunk, falling from ledge to ledge, from glass to
    glass.
I want the air around me to be invisible, resilient,
Able to flow past rocks.
I will carry the boulders with me to the valley.
Then ascending I will fall through space again:
Glittering in the sun, like the crystal in sideboards,
Goblets of the old life, before it was ruined by the Church.
And when I ascend the third time, I will fall forever,
Missing the earth entirely.

Hearing Men Shout at Night

on MacDougal Street

How strange to awake in a city,
And hear grown men shouting in the night!
On the farm the darkness wins,
And the small ones nestle in their graves of cold:
Here is a boiling that only exhaustion subdues,
A bitter moiling of muddy waters
At which the voices of white men feed!

The street is a sea, and mud boils up
When the anchor is lifted, for now at midnight there is about to
     sail
The first New England slave-ship with the Negroes in the hold.

The Current Administration

1

Here Morgan dies like a dog among whispers of angels;
The saint is born among tin cans in the orchard;
A rose receives the name of "The General Jackson."
Here snow-white blossoms bloom in the bare homes
Of bankmen, and with a lily the Pope meets
A delegation of waves, and blesses the associations
Of the ocean; I walk with a coarse body through winds
That carry the birds on their long roads to the poles,
And see the ghost of Locke above the railroad tracks.

2

Snow fell all night on a farmyard in Montana.
And the Assyrian lion blazed above the soybean fields.
The last haven of Jehovah, down from the old heavens,
Hugged a sooty corner of the murdered pine.
                              Arabic numerals
Walked the earth, dressed as bankers and sportsmen,
And at night diamonds in slippers invade our sleep.
Black beetles, bright as Cadillacs, toil down
The long dusty road into the mountains of South Dakota.

3

One night we find ourselves near the giant's house.
At dawn, mist blows over the great meadow.

Outside the steps, we find an aunt and uncle
Dead for twenty years working with hoes.
In their beds are small old men growing from the ground.
A mill grinding. We go in. Chairs
In the great room, hacked from redwood.
Tiny loaves of bread with ears lie on the President's table.
Steps coming! The Father will soon return!

Andrew Jackson's Speech

Dido to Aeneas: "I have broke faith with the ashes of Sichaeus!"

I heard Andrew Jackson say, as he closed his Virgil:

"The harsh ravishers in Detroit, inheritors of the soot
Of chimney boys, when they raised the mighty poor,
Broke faith with the cinders of Sichaeus.

"I shot to save the honour of my wife;
And I would shoot again, to save my people.
The Republic lies in the blossoms of Washington.

"The poor have been raised up by the Revolution.
Washington, riding in cold snow at Valley Forge,
Warned the poor never to take another husband."

His voice rose in the noisy streets of Detroit.

Sleet Storm on
the Merritt Parkway

I look out at the white sleet covering the still streets
As we drive through Scarsdale—
The sleet began falling as we left Connecticut,
And the winter leaves swirled in the wet air after cars
Like hands suddenly turned over in a conversation.
Now the frost has nearly buried the short grass of March.
Seeing the sheets of sleet untouched on the wide streets,
I think of the many comfortable homes stretching for miles,
Two and three stories, solid, with polished floors,
With white curtains in the upstairs bedrooms,
And small perfume flagons of black glass on the window sills,
And warm bathrooms with guest towels, and electric lights—
What a magnificent place for a child to grow up!
And yet the children end in the river of price-fixing,
Or in the snowy field of the insane asylum.
The sleet falls—so many cars moving toward New York—
Last night we argued about the Marines invading Guatemala in
    1947,
The United Fruit Company had one water spigot for 200 fami-
    lies,
And the ideals of America, our freedom to criticize,
The slave systems of Rome and Greece, and no one agreed.

III

The Vietnam War

After the Industrial Revolution,
All Things Happen at Once

Now we enter a strange world, where the Hessian Christmas
Still goes on, and Washington has not reached the other shore;
The Whiskey Boys
Are gathering again on the meadows of Pennsylvania
And the Republic is still sailing on the open sea.

I saw a black angel in Washington dancing
On a barge, saying, Let us now divide kennel dogs
And hunting dogs; Henry Cabot Lodge, in New York,
Talking of sugar cane in Cuba; Ford,
In Detroit, drinking mother's milk;
Henry Cabot Lodge, saying, "Remember the *Maine!*"
Ford, saying, "History is bunk!"
And Wilson saying, "What is good for General Motors . . ."

Who is it, singing? Don't you hear singing?
It is the dead of Cripple Creek;
Coxey's army
Like turkeys are singing from the tops of trees!
And the Whiskey Boys are drunk outside Philadelphia.

Asian Peace Offers

Rejected without Publication

These suggestions by Asians are not taken seriously.
We know Rusk smiles as he passes them to someone.
Men like Rusk are not men:
They are bombs waiting to be loaded in a darkened hangar.
Rusk's assistants eat hurriedly,
Talking of Teilhard de Chardin,
Longing to get back to their offices
So they can cling to the underside of the steel wings shuddering
    faintly in the high altitudes.
They land first, and hand the coffee cup to the drawn pilot.
They start the projector, and show the movie about the mad pro-
    fessor.

Lost angels huddled on a night branch!
The waves crossing
And recrossing beneath,
The sound of the rampaging Missouri,
Bending the reeds again and again—something inside us
Like a ghost train in the Rockies
About to be buried in snow!
Its long hoot
Making the owl in the Douglas fir turn his head . . .

War and Silence

The bombers spread out, temperature steady
A Negro's ear sleeping in an automobile tire
Pieces of timber float by saying nothing
*

Bishops rush about crying, There is no war,
And bombs fall,
Leaving a dust on the beech trees
*

One leg walks down the road and leaves
The other behind, the eyes part
And fly off in opposite directions
*

Filaments of death grow out.
The sheriff cuts off his black legs
And nails them to a tree

Counting Small-Boned Bodies

Let's count the bodies over again.

If we could only make the bodies smaller,
The size of skulls,
We could make a whole plain white with skulls in the moon-
    light!

If we could only make the bodies smaller,
Maybe we could get
A whole year's kill in front of us on a desk!

If we could only make the bodies smaller,
We could fit
A body into a finger-ring, for a keepsake forever.

As the Asian War Begins

There are longings to kill that cannot be seen,
Or are seen only by a minister who no longer believes in God,
Living in his parish like a crow in its nest.

And there are flowers with murky centers,
Impenetrable, ebony, basalt . . .

Conestogas go past, over the Platte, their contents
Hidden from us, murderers riding under the canvas . . .

Give us a glimpse of what we cannot see,
Our enemies, the soldiers and the poor.

At a March against the
Vietnam War

Washington, November 27, 1965

Newspapers rise high in the air over Maryland

We walk about, bundled in coats
        and sweaters in the late November sun

Looking down, I see feet moving
Calmly, gaily,
Almost as if separated from their bodies

But there is something moving in the dark somewhere
Just beyond
The edge of our eyes: a boat
Covered with machine guns
Moving along under trees

It is black,
The hand reaches out
And cannot touch it—
It is that darkness among pine boughs
That the Puritans brushed
As they went out to kill turkeys

At the edge of the jungle clearing
It explodes
On the ground

We long to abase ourselves

We have carried around this cup of darkness
We have longed to pour it over our heads

We make war
Like a man anointing himself

Hatred of Men with Black Hair

I hear voices praising Tshombe, and the Portuguese
In Angola, these are the men who skinned Little Crow!
We are all their sons, skulking
In back rooms, selling nails with trembling hands!

We distrust every person on earth with black hair;
We send teams to overthrow Chief Joseph's government;
We train natives to kill Presidents with blowdarts;
We have men loosening the nails on Noah's ark.

The State Department floats in the heavy jellies near the bottom
Like exhausted crustaceans, like squids who are confused,
Sending out beams of black light to the open sea,
Fighting their fraternal feeling for the great landlords.

We have violet rays that light up the jungles at night, showing
The friendly populations; we are teaching the children of ritual
To overcome their longing for life, and we send
Sparks of black light that fit the holes in the generals' eyes.

Underneath all the cement of the Pentagon
There is a drop of Indian blood preserved in snow:
Preserved from a trail of blood that once led away
From the stockade, over the snow, the trail now lost.

Driving through Minnesota
during the Hanoi Bombings

We drive between lakes just turning green;
Late June. The white turkeys have been moved
To new grass.
How long the seconds are in great pain!
Terror just before death,
Shoulders torn, shot
From helicopters, the boy
Tortured with the telephone generator,
"I felt sorry for him,
And blew his head off with a shotgun."
These instants become crystals,
Particles
The grass cannot dissolve. Our own gaiety
Will end up
In Asia, and in your cup you will look down
And see
Black Starfighters.
We were the ones we intended to bomb!
Therefore we will have
To go far away
To atone
For the sufferings of the stringy-chested
And the small rice-fed ones, quivering
In the helicopter like wild animals,
Shot in the chest, taken back to be questioned.

IV

In Praise of Grief

O dear children, look in what a dungeon we are lying, in
what lodging we are, for we have been captured by the spirit
of the outward world; it is our life, for it nourishes and
brings us up, it rules in our marrow and bones, in our flesh
and blood, it has made our flesh earthly, and now death has
us.

—Jacob Boehme

Melancholia

1

A light seen suddenly in the storm, snow
Coming from all sides, like flakes
Of sleep, and myself
On the road to the dark barn,
Halfway there, a black dog near me.

2

Light on the wooden rail.
Someone I knew and loved.
As we hear the dates of his marriage
And the years he moved,
A wreath of dark fir and shiny laurel
Slips off the coffin.

3

A cathedral: I see
Starving men, weakened, leaning
On their knees. But the bells ring anyway,
Sending out over the planted fields
A vegetation, sound waves with long leaves.

4

There is a wound on the trunk,
Where the branch was torn off.
A wind comes out of it,
Rising, swelling,
Swirling over everything alive.

Turning Away from Lies

1

If we are truly free, and live in a free country,
When shall I be without this heaviness of mind?
When shall I have peace? Peace this way and peace that way?
I have already looked beneath the street
And there I saw the bitter waters going down,
The ancient worms eating up the sky.

2

Christ did not come to redeem our sins
The Christ Child was not obedient to his parents
The Kingdom of Heaven does not mean the next life
No one in business can be a Christian
The two worlds are both in this world

3

The saints rejoice out loud upon their beds!
Their song moves through the troubled sea
The way the holy tortoise moves
From dark blue into troubled green,
Or ghost crabs move above the dolomite.
The thieves are crying in the wild asparagus.

A Home in Dark Grass

In the deep fall, the body awakes,
And we find lions on the seashore—
Nothing to fear.
The wind rises, the water is born,
Spreading white tomb-clothes on a rocky shore,
Drawing us up
From the bed of the land.

We did not come to remain whole.
We came to lose our leaves like the trees,
The trees that are broken
And start again, drawing up from the great roots;
Like mad poets captured by the Moors,
Men who live out
A second life.

That we should learn of poverty and rags,
That we should taste the weed of Dillinger,
And swim in the sea,
Not always walking on dry land,
And, dancing, find in the trees a saviour,
A home in dark grass,
And nourishment in death.

Looking at New-Fallen Snow
from a Train

Snow has covered the next line of tracks,
And filled the empty cupboards in the milkweed pods;
It has stretched out on the branches of weeds,
And softened the frost-hills, and the barbed-wire rolls
Left leaning against a fencepost—
It has drifted onto the window ledges high in the peaks of
      barns.

    A man throws back his head, gasps
    And dies. His ankles twitch, his hands open and close,
    And the fragment of time that he has eaten is exhaled from
        his pale mouth to nourish the snow.
    A salesman falls, striking his head on the edge of the
        counter.

Snow has filled out the peaks on the tops of rotted fence posts.
It has walked down to meet the slough water,
And fills all the steps of the ladder leaning against the eaves.
It rests on the doorsills of collapsing children's houses,
And on transformer boxes held from the ground forever in the
      center of cornfields.

A man lies down to sleep.
Hawks and crows gather around his bed.
Grass shoots up between the hawks' toes.
Each blade of grass is a voice.
The sword by his side breaks into flame.

In Danger from the Outer World

This burning in the eyes, as we open doors,
This is only the body burdened down with leaves,
The opaque flesh, heavy as November grass,
Growing stubbornly, triumphant even at midnight.

And another day disappears into the cliff,
And the Eskimos come to greet it with sharp cries—
The black water swells up over the new hole.
The grave moves forward from its ambush,

Moving over the hills on black feet,
Living off the country,
Leaving dogs and sheep murdered where it slept;
Some shining thing, inside, that has served us well

Shakes its bamboo bars—
It may be gone before we wake . . .

The Fire of Despair

Has Been Our Saviour

Today, autumn.
Heaven's roots are still.
O holy trees, rejoicing ruin of leaves,
How easily we see spring coming in your black branches!
Not like the Middle Ages! Then iron ringing iron
At dawn, chill wringing
The grass, clatter of saddles,
The long flight on borrowed stone
Into the still air sobered by the hidden joy of crows.

Or the Ice Age!
Another child dead,
Turning bone stacks for bones, sleeves of snow blowing
Down from above, no tracks in the snow, in agony
Man cried out—like the mad hog, pierced, again,
Again, by teeth-spears, who
Grew his horny scales
From sheer despair—instants
Finally leading out of the snowbound valley!

This autumn, I
Cannot find the road
That way: the things that we must grasp,
The signs, are gone, hidden by spring and fall, leaving

A still sky here, a dusk there,
A dry cornleaf in a field; where has the road gone? All
Trace lost, like a ship sinking,
Where what is left and what goes down both bring despair.
Not finding the road, we are slowly pulled down.

Looking at Some Flowers

Light is around the petals, and behind them:
Some petals are living on the other side of the light.
Like sunlight drifting onto the carpet
Where the casket stands, not knowing which world it is in.
And fuzzy leaves, hair growing from some animal
Buried in the green trenches of the plant.
Or the ground this house is on,
Only free of the sea for five or six thousand years.

V

A Body Not Yet Born

―――――――――

But when this had given me many a hard blow, doubtless from the Spirit that had a desire for me, I finally fell into great sadness and melancholy, when I viewed the great depth of this world, the sun and the stars and the clouds, rain and snow, and contemplated in my mind the whole creation of this world.

So then I found in all things good and evil, love and wrath, in creatures of reason as well as in wood, in stone, in earth, in the elements, in men and animals. Withal, I considered the little spark "man" and what it might be esteemed to be by God in comparison with this great work of heaven and earth.

In consequence I grew very melancholy, and what is written, though I knew it well, could not console me.

—Jacob Boehme

Looking into a Face

Conversation brings us so close! Opening
The surfs of the body,
Bringing fish up near the sun,
And stiffening the backbones of the sea!

I have wandered in a face, for hours,
Passing through dark fires.
I have risen to a body
Not yet born,
Existing like a light around the body,
Through which the body moves like a sliding moon.

Hurrying Away from the Earth

The poor, and the dazed, and the idiots
Are with us, they live in the casket of the sun
And the moon's coffin, as I walk out tonight
Seeing the night wheeling their dark wheelbarrow
All about the plains of heaven,
And the stars inexorably rising.
Dark moon! Sinister tears!
Shadow of slums and of the conquering dead!

Some men have pierced the chest with a long needle
To stop their heart from beating any more;
Another put blocks of ice in his bed
So he would die, women
Have washed their hair, and hanged themselves
In the long braids, one woman climbed
A high elm above her lawn,
Opened a box, and swallowed poisonous spiders. . . .

The time for exhortation is past. I have heard
The iron chairs scraping in asylums,
As the cold bird hunches into the winter
In the windy night of November.
The coal miners rise from their pits
Like a flash flood,
Like a rice field disintegrating.
Men cry when they hear stories of someone rising from the
    dead.

The Hermit

Darkness is falling through darkness,
Falling from ledge
To ledge.
There is a man whose body is perfectly whole.
He stands, the storm behind him,
And the grass blades are leaping in the wind.
Darkness is gathered in folds
About his feet.
He is no one. When we see
Him, we grow calm,
And sail on into the tunnels of joyful death.

A Journey with Women

1

Floating in turtle blood, going backward and forward,
We wake up like a mad sea-urchin
On the bloody fields near the secret pass—
There the dead sleep in jars . . .

2

Or we go at night slowly into the tunnels of the tortoise's claws,
Carrying chunks of the moon
To light the tunnels,
Listening for the sound of rocks falling into the sea . . .

3

Waking, we find ourselves in the tortoise's beak,
As he carries us high
Over New Jersey—going swiftly
Through the darkness between the constellations . . .

4

At dawn we are still transparent, pulling
In the starlight;
We are still falling like a room
Full of moonlight through the air . . .

Moving Inward at Last

The dying bull is bleeding on the mountain!
But inside the mountain, untouched
By the blood,
There are antlers, bits of oak bark,
Fire, herbs are thrown down.

When the smoke touches the roof of the cave,
The green leaves burst into flame,
The air of night changes to dark water,
The mountains alter and become the sea.

Riderless Horses

An owl on the dark waters
And so many torches smoking
By mossy stone
And horses that are seen riderless on moonlit nights
A candle that flutters as a black hand
Reaches out
All of these mean
A man with coins on his eyes

The vast waters
The cry of seagulls

Evolution from the Fish

This grandson of fishes holds inside him
A hundred thousand small black stones.
This nephew of snails, six feet long, lies naked on a bed
With a smiling woman, his head throws off light
Under marble, he is moving toward his own life
Like fur, walking. And when the frost comes, he is
Fur, mammoth fur, growing longer
And silkier, passing the woman's dormitory,
Kissing a stomach, leaning against a pillar,
He moves toward the animal, the animal with furry head!

What a joy to smell the flesh of a new child!
Like new grass! And this long man with the student girl,
Coffee cups, her pale waist, the spirit moving around them,
Moves, dragging a great tail into the darkness.
In the dark we blaze up, drawing pictures
Of spiny fish, we throw off the white stones!
Serpents rise from the ocean floor with spiral motions,
A man goes inside a jewel, and sleeps. Do
Not hold my hands down! Let me raise them!
A fire is passing up through the soles of my feet!

Wanting to Experience

All Things

The blind horse among the cherry trees—
And bones, sticking from cool earth.
The heart leaps
Almost up to the sky! But laments
And filaments pull us back into the darkness.
We cannot see—
But a paw
Comes out of the dark
To light the road. Suddenly I am flying,
I follow my own fiery traces through the night!

Opening an Oyster

We think of Charlemagne
As we open oysters.
Looking down, we see
Crowds waving from islands inside the oyster shell.
The neck swings to bite the dog.
When the fishermen take in the floats
They find nets some giant fish
Broke through at night.
At dusk we leave. We start north with twenty dogs.
A blizzard begins,
Making us look down.
And the miles of snow crust going past between the runners!
Westward the ice peaks
Like vast maternity hospitals turned white by oyster shells!
Going around the war hospital,
We see a pebble
That has drawn in the malignancy of the shark,
Like the mammoth hair
That melts an entire Russian county, drowning
Chickens and cows . . . then we know that in attics there are
Cloths folded that murdered the great princes!

When the Dumb Speak

There is a joyful night in which we lose
Everything, and drift
Like a radish
Rising and falling, and the ocean
At last throws us into the ocean,
And on the water we are sinking
As if floating on darkness.
The body raging
And driving itself, disappearing in smoke,
Walks in large cities late at night,
Or reading the Bible in Christian Science windows,
Or reading a history of Bougainville.
Then the images appear:
Images of death,
Images of the body shaken in the grave,
And the graves filled with seawater;
Fires in the sea,
The ships smoldering like bodies,
Images of wasted life,
Life lost, imagination ruined,
The house fallen,
The gold sticks broken,
Then shall the talkative be silent,
And the dumb shall speak.